1/02

DATE DUE

JUL 2-6-02			
JUN 05 02			
JUL 22 02			
DEC 04 02			
JUL 05 03			
OCT 11 2005			
11-2-05			
JAN 05 06			
MAY 22 09			
11/9/09			
GAYLORD			PRINTED IN U.S.A.

Source

Also by Mark Doty

Turtle, Swan (1987)

Bethlehem in Broad Daylight (1991)

My Alexandria (1993)

Atlantis (1995)

Heaven's Coast (1996)

Sweet Machine (1998)

Firebird (1999)

Still Life with Oysters and Lemon (2001)

poems

Source

Mark Doty

HarperCollins*Publishers*

HarperCollins books may be purchased for educational, business, or sales promotional use. For information, please write: Special Markets Department, HarperCollins Publishers Inc., 10 East 53rd Street, New York, NY 10022.

FIRST EDITION

Designed by Ann Heilmeier

Printed on acid-free paper

Library of Congress Cataloging-in-Publication Data is available upon request.

ISBN 0-06-621013-5

01 02 03 04 05 ❖/PC 10 9 8 7 6 5 4 3 2 1

Some of these poems have appeared, often in earlier versions, in the following publications:

THE ATLANTIC MONTHLY: *Lily and Bronze*

BLACK WARRIOR REVIEW: *Lost in the Stars*

THE BOSTON PHOENIX: *Fish R Us*

FIVE POINTS: *Letter to Walt Whitman*

THE GETTYSBURG REVIEW: *Source*

GULF COAST: *Hesperides Street*

LONDON REVIEW OF BOOKS: *Brian Age 7*
    Manhattan: Luminism
    Principalities of June
    Summer Landscape

PLOUGHSHARES: *Private Life*

POETRY REVIEW (UK):   *American Sublime*

SLATE: *At the Gym*
    Paul's Tattoo
    Sea Grape Valentine
    Catalina Macaw

SOLO: *Time on Main*

THE THREEPENNY REVIEW: *Elizabeth Bishop, Croton; watercolor, 9″ x 5¾″, n.d.*

TIN HOUSE: *To the Engraver of My Skin*
    Watermelon Soda

WASHINGTON SQUARE: *A Little Rabbit Dead in the Grass*

WITNESS: *Essay: The Love of Old Houses*

"Letter to Walt Whitman" was commissioned by BBC Radio Three and first read on the program Fan Mail in September 1997.

"An Island Sheaf" first appeared as a chapbook from The Dim Gray Bar Press, New York.

for Paul

The author is grateful to the Lila Wallace/Reader's Digest Fund for support that enabled the completion of these poems; gratitude as well to Lucie Brock-Broido, Alison Callahan, Bill Clegg, Carol Muske Dukes, Richard Howard, and Robert Jones.

Contents

A Little Rabbit Dead in the Grass   *1*

Fish R Us   *5*

At the Gym   *8*

Lost in the Stars   *10*

Manhattan: Luminism   *16*

Letter to Walt Whitman   *24*

Paul's Tattoo   *35*

Private Life   *38*

An Island Sheaf   *41*
  1. Sea Grape Valentine   *41*
  2. Watermelon Soda   *43*
  3. Elizabeth Bishop: *Croton*;
     watercolor, 9" x 5¾", n.d.   *44*
  4. Hesperides Street   *45*
  5. Catalina Macaw   *49*

Brian Age 7   *51*

Essay: The Love of Old Houses   *53*

To the Engraver of My Skin   *56*

Principalities of June   *58*

Summer Landscape   *60*

Lily and Bronze   *64*

After the Fourth   66

American Sublime   68

Time on Main   70

Source   73

Men and women crowding fast in the streets,
if they are not flashes and specks, what are they?

—WALT WHITMAN

Source

A Little Rabbit Dead in the Grass

All that was quick,
soul of dart and hurry.
    No soul now,

and still the body
—not even the length
    of my hand—

seems poised
for springing, legs
    jutting forward

and back as if
in mid-leap . . .
    And here comes

the *So?* of poetry:
just one bunny dead
    of mysterious causes,

one among legion,
though this particular
    shocks, early,

in the frosty grass
by the kitchen door,
    where each

specific blade
makes as always
        the carpeting text

of their journey-
work, the old blab
        of the grass's book.

Everything and nothing,
the page says, though
        you turn it

round and round, *each
and all,* though you can't help
        set yourself

the task of explication,
the elegist's thankless work:
So long, so what?

Once only, these two
shoe-black pupils
        —though behind

the daylight's a pressure
of new rabbits,
        reinforcements

eager to arrive.
Animals: themselves
        and nothing but

an instance of some
more general rule.
        Beloved because

we can almost bear it?
And therefore love them more,
    how each dog's any,

every lemon-scaled
fandango in the restaurant tank
    the perfect incarnation

of carp? Couldn't you
be happy with that?
    No, says the *so;*

no rest for the *so.*
Shiva built the world,
    the story goes,

on a single syllable,
heavenly irritant,
    and the pearl

of reality grew;
imagine *so* right
    at the heart

of the world.
My littlest question,
    curve of the sibilant

sliding into the aperture
of O: brief uncrackable
    syllable—

which seems to flicker
in the oystery gleam
    of the ears,

narrower than thumbtips,
and on the minute,
    eraser-colored nose

(artfully crafted thing!),
and on the slender brow,
    where some trace

of thought seems written.

Fish R Us

Clear sac
of coppery eyebrows
suspended in amnion,
not one moving—

A Mars,
composed entirely
of single lips,
each of them gleaming—

this bag of fish
(have they actually
traveled here like *this*?)
bulges while they

acclimate, presumably,
to the new terms
of the big tank
at Fish R Us. Soon

they'll swim out
into separate waters,
but for now they're
shoulder to shoulder

in this clear and
burnished orb, each fry
about the size of this line,
too many lines for any

bronzy antique epic,
a million of them,
a billion incipient citizens
of a goldfish Beijing,

a São Paulo,
a Mexico City.
They seem to have sense
not to move but hang

fire, suspended, held
at just a bit of distance
(a bit is all there is), all
facing outward, eyes

(they can't even blink)
turned toward the skin
of the sac they're in,
this swollen polyethylene.

And though nothing's
actually rippling but their gills,
it's still like looking up
into falling snow,

if all the flakes
were a dull, breathing gold,
as if they were streaming
toward—not us, exactly,

but what they'll be . . .
Perhaps they're small enough
—live sparks, for sale
at a nickel apiece—

that one can actually
see them transpiring:
they want to swim
forward, want to

eat, want to take place.
Who's going to know
or number or even see them all?

They pulse in their golden ball.

At the Gym

This salt-stain spot
marks the place where men
lay down their heads,
back to the bench,

and hoist nothing
that need be lifted
but some burden they've chosen
this time: more reps,

more weight, the upward shove
of it leaving, collectively,
this sign of where we've been:
shroud-stain, negative

flashed onto the vinyl
where we push something
unyielding skyward,
gaining some power

at least over flesh,
which goads with desire,
and terrifies with frailty.
Who could say who's

added his heat to the nimbus
of our intent, here where
we make ourselves:
something difficult

lifted, pressed or curled,
Power over beauty,
power over power!
Though there's something more

tender, beneath our vanity,
our will to become objects
of desire: we sweat the mark
of our presence onto the cloth.

Here is some halo
the living made together.

Lost in the Stars

The Café Musicale,
a benefit organized by Billy—
sweet, irksome Billy,
who seemed fundamentally
incapable of organizing anything,
though he'd managed

to fill a hall, a midwinter Saturday,
the town muffled by snow,
and dozens ready to perform:
girl singers with severely sculptural hair,
earnest poets, West End Wendy,
who played cowgirl tunes

on her ukulele, and a pianist
who'd driven all the way from a lounge
where he was appearing in Hyannis.
Where did Billy find us all?
The cause: PWAs, a fund
for art supplies, paint and clay

and darkroom chemicals.
We filled the folding chairs;
act after act the snow piled up
outside, scrolling the windows
with an intimate, tumbling rhythm,
ethereal. Marie read poems,

and Michael—in a thrift-store retro
ensemble that meant *I want a boyfriend*—
made his literary debut.
Someone played the spoons.
Davíd, who'd said our town
averaged that year a funeral a week,

did a performance piece
about the unreliability of language.
Someone showed slides: family snapshots
tinted the colors of a bruise. (Art heals,
we thought. It was 1992,
and we were powerless.)

We were studiedly casual
in our clothes, which is why
the drag queen who appeared,
at intermission, startled so:
black glittery leotard, eyelashes
spiking from kohl-rimmed, huge

black eyes, bouffant hard
and black, high thick heels:
it was a wonder she'd come out of the snow.
When she took the stage,
the houselights—though
there were none—dimmed.

The music was Kurt Weill,
"Lost in the Stars." Nothing
overtly funny about it:
since she *was* irony
she did nothing ironic,
only a raised eyebrow,

a subtle turn of the wrist
to acknowledge the ways
the limits of flesh
resisted her ambitions.
A long time, in those lyrics,
before "I" appears,

to tell us the chanteuse
has wandered her way
toward disenchantment:
I've been walking through
the night and the day,
she sang, *and sometimes*

it seems maybe God's
gone away, not without
a certain warmth in those tones,
not without wisdom.
(He is unpossessed
of any special understanding,

daytimes, off work, but she
was a contained storm,
her body's darkness opening,
as if one of the windows
had fallen open, startling us
with that continuous scrolling freefall.)

Then those who'd left someone
home in bed, someone not well enough
to come, began to tug on scarves
and coats. And the half-dozen
who'd been helped to their metal chairs,
canes leaning against them,

men with portals in their necks
or chests for foscarnet
and gancyclovir, who'd clapped
or nodded off while
we raised money for art supplies—
they all went home too.

I walked into the snow
(*I've been walking through
the night and the day*);
Wally was home in bed blocks away—
sleeping, I hoped, though I'd left him
alone as long as I dared.

I can hardly remember how
it felt now, that relentless
hopelessness. The Musicale,
in the way of such things,
went on long after it was over,
and the next year there was another,

though Billy'd begun to unravel
then, his introductions less sensible,
his imitations of his friends opaque.
No one had the heart
to tell him to sit down.
We'd stay through it;

we'd stay for Billy,
and to buy the men we knew
clay and brushes and sketching paper.
How will I remember them?
I wouldn't have guessed
it would be this: how

—dark and glittering and
strangely self-contained—
she reached her gloved hand
toward us (*We're lost*)
in a gesture unmistakably twofold:
she wanted to touch us,

and we were already,
in her lyric, contained.
This is what imagination
must do, isn't it, find a form?
She dazzled our estrangement.
She asserted her night.

She was the no one we needed;
she sang the necessary
gleaming emptiness.
You who were taken,
you who are gone now
in the drift and ash of the lyric

we've made of you,
gone into the snowfall
still unreeling somewhere,
repetitive, poised, so relentless
you might take it for stillness,
how will we remember you?

The black glove opens
and there it is, still falling,
beyond memory, beyond recovery,
the snow of 1992.

I have a saucepan of Billy's, still; he made a stew for me when Wally died. He spent a whole afternoon seasoning it: parsley, rosemary, oregano. And Peter, at Billy's memorial, was so true to the memory of his friend he seemed almost too exasperated to cry, as if among the thousand irritating things Billy would do, now he'd gone and died. And the best way to keep something of Billy was to hold on to how much he'd annoyed us: in that way we could remember who he was.

Manhattan: Luminism

The sign said *immunology*
but I read
illuminology: and look,

heaven *is* a platinum latitude
over Fifth, fogged result
of sun on brushed

steel, pearl
dimensions. Cézanne:
"We are an iridescent chaos."

Balcony over Lexington, May evening,

fog-wreath'd towers,
gothic dome lit from within,
monument of our aspirations

turned hollow, abandoned

somehow. And later, in the florist's window
on Second Avenue, a queen's display
of orchid and fern, lush heap

of dried sheaves, bounty of grasses . . .

What's that? Mice
far from any field
but feasting.

◆

The sign said
K YS MADE,
but what will op n,

if the locksmith's
lost his vowel
—his entrance,

edge, his means
of egress—
which held together

the four letters
of his trade?
City of consonants,

city of locks,
and he's lost
the E.

◆

(A Mirror in the Chelsea Hotel)

Here, where odd old things have come to rest
—a lamp that never meant
to keep on going, a chest
whose tropical veneers
are battered and submissive—

this glass gives the old hotel room
back to itself in a warmer atmosphere,
as if its silver were thickening,
a gathering opacity held here,
just barely giving back . . .

This mirror resists what it can,
too weary for generosity.
As if each coming and going,
each visitor turned, one night
or weeks, to check a collar

or the angle of a hat, left some residue,
a bit of leave-taking preserved in mercury.
And now, filled up with all that regard,
there is hardly any room for regarding,
and a silvered fog fills nearly all

the space, like rain: the city's lovely,
crowded dream, which closes you
into itself like a folding screen.

Almost nightfall, West 82nd,
and a child falls to her knees
on the cement, and presses

herself against the glass
of the video store,
because she wants to hold her face

against the approaching face,
huge, open, on the poster
hung low in the window,

down near the sidewalk:
an elephant walking toward
the viewer, ears wide to the world.

She cries out in delight,
at first, and her mother
acknowledges her pleasure,

but then she's still there,
kneeling, in silence, and no matter
what the mother does or says

the girl's not moving,
won't budge, though her name's
called again and again.

Could you even name it,
that longing—which suddenly seems
to rule these streets,

as if the underlying principle
of the city had been drawn up
from beneath the pavement

by a girl who doesn't know
any better than to insist
on the force of her wish

to look into the gaze which seems
to go on steadily coming toward her,
though of course it isn't moving at all.

◆

I woke in the old hotel.
The shutters were open
in the high, single window;
the light gone delicate, platinum.
What had I been dreaming,

what would become of me now?
There were doves calling,
their three-note tremolo
climbing the airshaft
—something about the depth

of that sound, where it reaches in you,
what it touches. You've been abraded,
something exchanged or given away
with every encounter, on the street,
the train, something of you lost

to the bodies that unnerved you,
in the station, streaming ahead,
everyone going somewhere certain
in the randomly intersecting flow
of our hurry, until you could be anyone,

in the furious commingling . . .
But now you're more awake, aren't you,
and of course these aren't doves,
not in the middle of Manhattan;
a little harsher, more driven,

these pigeons, though recognizable
still in the pulse of their throats
the threnody of their kind, rising
to you or to that interior ear
with which you are always listening,

in the great city, where things are said
to no one, and everyone, and still
it's the same . . . You were afraid
you were edgeless, one bit
of light's indifferent streaming,

and you are—but in a way you also
are singled out, are, in the old sense,
a soul, because you have heard
the thrilling, deep-entering rumple
and susurrus of the birds, and now

a little cadence of sun in motion
on the windowsill's bricked edge,
where did it come from?
Moving with the same ripple . . . As if,
audible in the ragged yearning,

visible in this tentative assertion of sun
on the lip of a window in Chelsea,
is a flake of that long waving
long ago lodged in you. All this light
traveled aeons to become 23rd Street,

and a hotel room in the late afternoon
—the singular neon outside already
warm and quavering—and you in it,
sure now, because of the song
being delivered to you, dealt to you

like an outcome, that there is
something stubborn in us
—does it matter how small it is?—
that does not diminish.
What is it? An ear, a wave?

Not our histories or who we love
or certainly our faces, which dissolve
even as we're living. Not a bud
or a cinder, not a seed
or a spark: something else:

obdurate, specific, insoluble.
Something in us does not erode.

Letter to Walt Whitman

Are you more than editions, or the grave's
uncondition'd hair? (More likely, these days,
permed and mowed to chemical perfection.)
I hope this finds you. I know you've been bothered

all century, poets lining up
to claim lineage. And not just poets—
in a photobook, brand-new,
handsome lads wrestle in sepia,

freshly laved by some historic stream:
the roughs are models now, and pose
in nothing on the opposite pages from stanzas
of your verse: a twentieth-century

letter to you. As are the scrawls
beneath the underpass, ruby and golden
cuneiform reinscribed on train-car sides:
songs of me and my troops, spray-painted

to our prophet, who enjoins us to follow
—what else?—our own lights,
intuitions glimmered in the body's
liquid meshes, our own

and the bodies beside us . . .
I am so far from you, Uncle, yet
in this way emboldened:
Last summer, in the year of our _____

nineteen hundred ninety-six, Paul and I
drove to Camden, where your house still stands
—modest, clapboard, dwarfed by the prison
glowering across the street, where trucks shock

themselves percussively on outrageous
potholes. Jail, detox, welfare: Camden
accepts it all, Camden's the hole in which
we throw anything, neighborhood so torched

it doesn't even have a restaurant.
You dwelt here, honored, half-confined, hailed
in your bed as a sage by a country
you helped to misunderstand you.

I get ahead of myself, Walt; the docent
unbolted the door to your manila rooms,
honey of June sun through shades the tint
of old newsprint: We loved the evidence of you,

fired by that filtering amber,
even while the swoops of car alarms
decibeled outside, and rips and crashes
by the curb made us sure our car'd

been stripped to the chassis.
Here your backpack, crumpled like a leather
sigh; a bit of your handwriting, framed;
a menu for a testimonial, and far too many

photos of your tomb: the stuff of image,
useless pomp in which you readily
partook—was this what we'd come to see?
Then one thing made you seem alive:

your parrot, Walt, friend of the last years,
a hand-span tall, lusters preserved
by the taxidermist's wax, or the case
in which he perched, or feathers' sheer

propensity to last. Your bird,
who ate from your own hand! And sat astride
your shoulder while you read the mail.
On whose bright eye's skim (glass now,

liquid original long lost to time)
curved this room, light through
—could they have been?—these shades,
while you crooked a finger to chuck

his ruffed neck. He's jaunty, brave,
his painted jungle gloamed in darkening
linseed, head crooked toward the future,
ambiguous as a construction by Cornell . . .

I thought if I leaned near that glass I bent,
patriarch, closer to you—he had
had your ear, didn't he, and if I leaned
toward his still-inquiring, precious eye . . .

I hardly heard the racket outside,
diminishing tremolo of sirens, names
the boys broke, laughing, as a bottle smashed:
I bent toward your glassed companion

still these ninety years in his sealed vitrine;
suddenly I seemed to see, tender, as if
I could smell it, Walt, powdered, warm,
the skin of your neck . . . Granted

this intimacy, I have some questions
for you. Did you mean it?
Democratic America joined by
delight in the beauty of boys,

especially working-class ones? I joke.
I know you meant adhesiveness,
that bond of flesh to equal flesh,
might be the bedrock of an order,

a compact founded on skin's durable,
knowable flame. I've felt what I think
you meant. I don't mean to romance this, Walt,
but much of what I've known of fellowship

I've apprehended in the basest church,
—where we're seldom dressed, and the affable
equality among worshippers is
sometimes like your democratic vista,

men held in common by our common skin.
But it doesn't take sex to understand:
once, in a beach side changing shed packed
with men, all girths and degrees of furred

and smooth, firm and softened, fish-belly
to warm rose to midnight's dimmest spaces
between stars, sunburnt on my bench, waiting
my turn in the mist of shower steam,

I thought, *We're all here, every one of us,*
the men of the world in the men's house, nude,
buffed with towels, young men and old
and boys bathing together, so much flesh

in one place it seemed to be of the soul . . .
As if I stood in that fogged, original room
through which each individual enters
the world, and each of us, nameless, already

in the body that would be ourselves,
was awaiting his turn. So we stood
in sympathy, since we understood
our fellows would suffer, knew

we were entering upon our singular,
shared lot . . . And I can understand
how you might base on that a nation,
Walt, though each of us left the warm

and darkened shed in separate clothes,
in separate cars, which drained out
of the parking lot onto the blacktop
and the expressway back to the city,

headed home to the song of my self, self,
self. That moment, unguarded,
skin to skin, why didn't it make us change?

. . . I have been interrupted here

by two Jehovah's Witnesses—
men in skinny neckwear with a boy in tow,
his dad's blond miniature—knocking
with millennial threats and promises.

I was not polite. Our poets fear
the didactic, the sweeping claim; we let
the televangelists and door-to-door
preachers talk hope and apocalypse

while we tend more private gardens. You saw
shattered soldier boys bound up in their beds,
lost your day job for writing scandalous
verse; you knew no one would base a world

upon what you believed: incendiary,
peculiar, nothing a "good gray poet"
could avow. Imagine being called *that*,
imagine *liking* it . . . Your little parrot's

ghost tweaks my ear, cautionary note:
How could I know the price you had to pay,
what you had to say to get away with
your astonishing news: no conflation,

you made it plain, to mistake the nipple
for the soul, souse of ejaculate
for the warm rain of heaven. It stops
my breath, to think of what you said.

How? You answer as the dead do,

I write you now from Columbus,
Ohio, the fourteenth floor, hotel tower
attached to a convention center

bland as a tomb, though the simile
lends a gravity actuality lacks:
acres of carpet, humming fluorescent tubes,
buoyed air, all of it waiting for someone

to sell somebody something. It's Sunday.
I'm a visiting poet here, currently
off duty. I'd like you to see my view:
candescent sky, fueled with orange plumes

and smudgings of a darkling plum,
one of Rothko's brooding visions
of what Moses heard, all spread over
the financial district of Columbus,

which just now I find strangely lovely.
Down there in the nearly vacant civic
plazas a few figures hurry against
a vicious spring wind, random Ohioans,

black sparks from an original flame. *Men
and women crowding fast in the streets, if
they are not flashes and specks* . . .

And now I write from home, most of the day

gone. Paul's done the laundry, and downstairs
on the couch reads Proust. Soon we'll go out
for Vietnamese. We have what amounts
to marriage—sexy, serviceable, pleasant,

plain. You might have lived like this
awhile with Peter Doyle, who now can say?
Of our company in your century,
dust and silence almost all erase.

I wonder if you'd like those boys
in underpants looming huge on billboards
over Seventh Avenue? We're freer now,
and move from ghetto to turbid mainstream.

And—explain this to a ghost!—our theorists
question notions of identity: Are you who you love,
or can you dwell in categorical ambiguity?
Our numbers divide, merge and multiply;

shoulder to shoulder with our fellow folk,
who's to say just who anyone is? You
couldn't have imagined how many of us,
—not just men who love men, I mean

all our uncountable specks and flares,
powerless, uncertain . . . You would not
like it here, despite the grassy persistence
of your name: I've crossed the Walt Whitman Bridge,

PA to Jersey, past Walt Whitman High,
even stopped on the Turnpike at
(denigration of our brightest hopes)
the Walt Whitman Service Area: shakes

and fries, the open freeway splitting what's left
of your American night, red sparks thrown
from semi windows arced in Independence Day
contrails . . . What could it mean,

for a vision to come true? Not
the child's-dream polychrome
of those Jehovah's Witness tracts—
happy people in sparkling nature,

a sparkling city welcoming. Poems
are written on the back of time,
inscriptions on the wrong side of a photograph:
scribbled flourish of our possibility.

Is it true then, what your descendant said,
that poetry makes nothing happen?
Just yesterday we worked in the garden,
earliest spring, brave sky, our apricot

newly burst into the first of seven
burning days. (When I saw a comet
from a plane, ancient tail a slurred flame,
it trailed these petals' icy double

through the midnight air.) We took off our shirts,
raked the dregs of leaves, glad for sun,
Uncle, while slender bees worried the blooms
in sun-buzzed endeavoring. We drove

to Fred Meyer, a sort of omnistore,
for saline solution, gym shorts, a rake.
In the big store's warmth and open embrace
who could I think of but you? We were

Americans there—working, corporate,
bikers, fancy wives, Hispanic ladies
with seriously loaded shopping carts,
one deftly accessorized crossdresser,

Indian kids in the ruins of their inheritance,
loading up on Easter candy, all of us standing,
khakis to jeans, in the bond of our common needs.
You wrote the book against which we are read.

Every one that sleeps is beautiful,
you said. Every one who shops is
also lovely: we go out together
to try on what the world is made of,

to accommodate all that bounty,
to praise and appraise, to see what's new.
As if to purchase were to celebrate.
I stand close with the other shoppers

each in turn, I dream in my dream
all the dreams . . . Who could be hopeful
for the sheer ascending numbers of us,
the poisoned sky and trees? Still I thought

of our apricot's upright, brandished flame,
scintillation held to the face of heaven,
new bees about their work
as though there'd never been a winter.

You answer me as the dead do.
And the poem stops here, Walt, while Paul
and I load the car with more than we ever
thought we'd need, white plastic bags flapping

in the breeze—the poems stops here,
in the parking lot, waiting for you.

Paul's Tattoo

The flesh dreams toward permanence,

and so this red carp noses from the inked dusk
of a young man's forearm as he tilts

the droning burin of his trade toward
the blank page of my dear one's biceps

—a scene framed, from where I watch,
in an arched mirror, a niche of mercuried glass

the shape of those prosceniums in which still lifes
reside, in cool museum rooms: tulips and medlars,

oysters and snails and flies on permanently
perishing fruit: vanitas. All *is* vanitas,

for these two arms—one figured, one just beginning
to be traced with the outline of a heart—

are surrounded by a cabinet of curiosities,
the tattooist's reflected shelves of skulls

—horses, pigs?—and photos of lobes and nipples
shocked into style. Trappings of evil

unlikely to convince: the shop's called 666,
a casket and a pit bull occupy the vestibule,

but the coffin's pink and the hellhound licked
our faces clean as the latex this bearded boy donned

to prick the veil my lover's skin presents
—rent, now, with a slightly comic heart,

warmly ironic, lightly shaded, and crowned,
as if to mean feeling's queen or king of any day,

certainly this one, a quarter-hour
suddenly galvanized by a rippling electric trace

firing adrenaline and an odd sense of limit
defied. Not overcome, exactly; this artist's

filled his shop with evidence of that.
To what else do these clean,

Dutch-white bones testify?
But resistant, still, skin grown less subject

to change, ruled by what is drawn there:
a freshly shadowed *corazón*

now heron-dark, and ringed
by blue exultant bits of sweat or flame—

as if the self contained too much
to be held, and flung out droplets

from the dear proud flesh
—stingingly warm—a steadier hand

has raised into art, or a wound,
or both. The work's done,

our design complete. A bandage,
to absorb whatever pigment

the newly writ might weep,
a hundred guilders, a handshake, back out

onto the street. Now all his life
he wears his heart beneath his sleeve.

Private Life

Little Kaiser, the parrot
in our local headshop's sidewalk cage,
confronts an unceasing daily stream
of whistles and coos and hellos,

waspish buzz of film on auto-wind,
the sudden, minor lightning
of a flash. He doesn't seem to mind.
Not a headshop exactly:

years ago the police swept away
the ranks of bongs and rolling papers,
leaving behind sex toys
and a universe of tie-dye arrayed

beside every conceivable kind
of bead; the tourists stream in,
in search of something wild,
and everyone looks, at least,

at Kaiser's cage; he chews
his parrot toys, he speaks,
or rocks from side to side
behind a sign that reads,

I bite. He couldn't be said to be
lonely; all day the world comes to him,
endless procession of faces,
only a few of them known.

We pass him every day.
Irascible acrobat, he's half the time
upside down, marvelous feet
commandeering the narrow wires,

or hanging from his roof,
lost in thought till he looks out
and begins his coloratura tape-loop
of whistles, cut-and-paste

of copycat cries: bicycle bells,
miaows, squeaky brakes, a brilliant
rendering of a cell phone's trill,
low in the throat. In the evening,

he's still there, up late, clicking
and preening at his oyster gleam.
(He is an African gray,
which means his modest cloak

is lined, beneath the tail, in stunning red,
a frank indulgence of the private life.)
Tonight it's chilly, late in the season,
bedtime soon. What does Kaiser dream?

Probably no original paradise;
this little trooper was born in a shop.
A soulmate, come to him
out of the daily stream? Why

should he prefer a single,
perfect other? Maybe he'd rather
give and give himself away;
maybe the pilgrim line of visitants

continues in the echoing landscape
of his night, one human form
after another bent over him
in momentary delight, while he takes

their measure, and mouths
a limited vocabulary,
all greeting and praise:
Hello, Pretty, Howdedo,

speech enough for our dear,
promiscuous singer, whose tongue
lifts and curls out to the world, performing
all night in his blanketed cage.

An Island Sheaf

Key West

I. Sea Grape Valentine

Loose leaf:
golden
fire-streams

branching into bayous
of darker flame,
breaking apart

near the rim
to finer, finer veins:
unnavigable Amazonia

in the shape of a heart
—a real heart, dear,
not the idealized kind,

and thus all throb
and trouble, and fallen
as if to remind us

we're fire at the core,
various heats.

Though everything

mottles,
at this latitude:
fruit and flower

and once-pink
porch columns,
even the puddle

between the bakery
and Kingdom Hall
giving up thunderhead

and rainbow, even
the concrete pier
a slow study

in corrosion's arts:
nothing unchecked
or unstippled

(old pink taxi
rusting in the sun),
nothing simple or im-

pervious to decay:
why not
this fallen valentine,

candybox token
veined in hot gold,
its tropic wax

embalmed and blazing?

2. Watermelon Soda

Pink scuttle
(a roasted pink,
like pork

in Chinese restaurants):
these claws poke out
from the pull-top

opening
of an empty can
of watermelon soda,

which clicks along
the sidewalk,
wobbling cylindrical

and alarming
beneath weary palms
accustomed to

the homeless.
Strange island,
to yield a walking

hot-pink soda can
inhabited by a lucky,
Modernist crab,

carrying on his back
a tropic shelter
by Barragán

or Le Corbusier,
perennially modish
if not quite practical,

since the candy-pink
pop can tips
and gyros

as he proceeds,
unstable island
—housed in style,

or hobbled by it?
The pink metal
flashes in the sun,

and seems worth it.
Or did yesterday.
This morning, after

the all-night storm,
where's he gone, our exile?
Floated clean away.

3. Elizabeth Bishop,
        Croton; watercolor, 9" x 53/4", n.d.

Exiles see exiles everywhere.

And so this leaf's solo,
enisled, its embered coral
barred with freckles of tropic
sable, bits of the lushest darkness
north of Havana. Not *far* north,

though; this little archipelago's
flush chromatics require
sea-light on humid acres
sun-worried to fecundity
and decay. How bright

a homeless one appears,
detached from context,
quickened by singularity!
Castaway not to be rescued,
not needing to go home, really;

this lonesome leaf's a study
never finished, since
we aren't sure what *one*
of anything is. And therefore
must begin the work again—

Try: this elliptical isle's coral
and aglow, beautifully barred
with lesser islands' tropic sable.
Try: this lonesome leaf's islanded,
autobiographical. Or:

Enisled, this ellipse is coral & sable . . .

4. Hesperides Street

I bought a can of coffee
—*por el gusto Latino*—
roasted on Hesperides Street, and saw

as soon as I read the label
an unlikely intersection: earthly sidewalks
cracked and unrolling beside the trees

of paradise, golden sun-apples
hung above the pitted asphalt
of a wonky part of town.

Sheer daydreaming,
there in the aisle
of Fausto's Food Palace

until I realized the heaven-street
I dreamed was, only slightly transposed,
the avenue of our December rental

—a cottage in a neighborhood where
we're neither welcome or not, simply not
at home. Even the taxis are pink,

and the rain relaxed; it has forever to fall,
punctuated, occasionally, by roosters
(who think it's dawn because it's cloudy)

and the squawk of what?
Two ibis walk wet asphalt.
Delicious unfamiliarity,

extended syllabics: guayabera
falling in the yard, poisonwood,
poinciana, the farfetched

gumbo-limbo. Unlikely intersection:
walking home from Fausto's,
half intent on the notion of heaven,

here is Kingdom Hall,
stuccoed that soft ubiquitous pink,
and here the Sunday-morning rush

at the Cuban bakery, hundred-pound
flour sacks stacked in the shop window
perpetually diminishing

and replenished, white dust
forever descending like a blessing.
Though we prefer next door,

the San Lázaro, which serves
the hottest *café con leche*
in big white cups of—regrettably—

styrofoam. All day men smoke
and drink *buchos* on the benches
and configure in their talk the paradise

to which exile must always refer,
their Havana. Any kingdom's imagined,
must be, before it's inhabited,

and heaven must be dreamed
as Cuba is: Is there a bakery there,
or sunny interstices among the palm fronds,

or the strange dignity of the traveler's tree,
or anyone like the diminutive cook at San Lazáro,
utterly silent under his halo of whitish hair,

who brews our morning coffee,
ladling more of his marvelous sugar
than I want to see? Peculiar intersections:

hounds and pink scooters, a hog
meditating in the arena of her pen,
abandoned high heels on a saggy stoop,

herons and pelicans and frigate birds
wheeling over our corner
—home to an ancient live oak

looming right beside
the Tree of Life Church of God,
and a likely candidate for the title:

roots upheaving the sidewalk,
a dozen fishline beards of Spanish moss
hung before the chapel's plain windows

—which glow, service nights,
unfigured, empty fields of green,
as though it were a relief to be freed

of images. Dear oxymoron,
Hesperides Street.
Heaven to earth?

That means love the rot black
in the tree-trunk crack,
and the corn snake—pink, what else—

fallen from soursop to sidewalk
in the ecstasy of swallowing a rat
so large it must dislocate its jaw

to admit the beloved thing.
Love the iridescent gas leaked
in a puddle poxed by easygoing rain,

orange peel and chicken bones,
discarded coffee cups sticky with milk
and three sugars, delicious, buzzed by wasps,

a dozen stray cats slipping in
and out a hole in the pink bricks
of the church foundation.

Heaven is here, and horrifying.
Does that mean it isn't heaven?
Ask the snake in the swoon

of his delirium, ask the gasoline
doing the rain some glamorous damage,
or scud-clouds worrying the pier

where the homeless stack their bags
and blankets, and one black man reclines
on a reclaimed chaise of a mattress,

and lays out daily,
for no reason I can figure,
a row of graduated coconuts

—demonstration of bounty,
hard and gold and green?
Ask San Lázaro, who blesses perpetually,

decked in his permanent wounds,
patron of the poor, and sick,
and sweet strong coffee:

heaven on earth is a lot of trouble,
but warm, and available, free—
or the price of a winter rental.

5. Catalina Macaw

Dürer painted a wing like this
—but only one, to imply
a whole too splendid

to render, or ask
that we visualize
what extends

this fierce lemon-
and-orient-sapphire
stretched toward

whatever it is
sublimity points to.
Though Bubba's no angel,

—she bit out the bars
of her cage!—
and attitude flashes

in her rapidly contracting
and pulsing eye,
flickering dot of pupil.

Are you the one
whom my soul seeks,
she seems to telegraph

in alert and eager Morse,
are you my tireless
companion,

the faithful other?
Pulse. Ruffle
of the feather-shallows.

No? Well then, *cracker?*

Brian Age 7

Grateful for their tour
of the pharmacy,
the first-grade class
has drawn these pictures,
each self-portrait taped
to the window-glass,
faces wide to the street,
round and available,
with parallel lines for hair.

I like this one best: Brian,
whose attenuated name
fills a quarter of the frame,
stretched beside impossible
legs descending from the ball
of his torso, two long arms
springing from that same
central sphere. He breathes here,

on his page. It isn't craft
that makes this figure come alive;
Brian draws just balls and lines,
in wobbly crayon strokes.
Why do some marks
seem to thrill with life,
possess a portion
of the nervous energy
in their maker's hand?

That big curve of a smile
reaches nearly to the rim
of his face; he holds
a towering ice cream,
brown spheres teetering
on their cone,
a soda fountain gift
half the length of him
—as if it were the flag

of his own country held high
by the unadorned black line
of his arm. Such naked support
for so much delight! Artless boy,
he's found a system of beauty:
he shows us pleasure
and what pleasure resists.
The ice cream is delicious.
He's frail beside his relentless standard.

Essay: The Love of Old Houses

A glow from rough-planed floorboards
knotted and grained and chestnut-hued,
and flecked in the pores with bits
of antique paint: whale oil and lead

for red; was it arsenic that made this green?
Remnants grace the pitted spots
where the sander wouldn't reach—
well, it could have, but what we wanted,

when we took the burr wheel's
unwieldy drum to these planks,
was to honor the whorls and curves
that made them themselves, variant,

well-used. Like skin. Fired just now
by afternoon pouring heat and honey
onto these wide swathes seasoned,
two centuries, to something durable,

too much an inhabitation of warmth
to qualify as inanimate—as though sunlight
softened their cooled, human store
and sent it wafting up like scent

from warmed wax. I know.
I am that firing light, and I'm the hand
that's oiled these boards
with a resin-and-varnish brew,

tincture that let these cello depths
emerge, and last. And so
what I've—we've—made is not
outside myself, not exactly;

rather it's a container—
sagging and shored, corroding
and replenished—in which one
doesn't need to hold oneself together:

relax, and oh, the rooms will do it for you.
It's safe to loosen our borders
here, and know ourselves housed.
I sanded and Danish-oiled

these floors with a man who's dead,
and the planks gleam still—
a visible form of vitality—
for you and I, love, who now revise,

as each inhabitant must,
the dwelling place. Making new
builds upon every layer come before;
we're joined to whoever

wore the stairstep down, or cracked
the corner of a windowpane, or waxed
these boards when company was coming.
Which is why I like old houses best:

here it's proved that time requires
a deeper, better verb than *pass*;
it's more like pool, and ebb, and double
back again, my history, his, yours,

subsumed into the steadying frame
of a phrase I love: *a building:*
both noun and verb, where we live
and what we do: fill it with ourselves,

all the way to the walls,
proximity made bearable by separate,
commingling privacies
that spill and meet at the edge

as clouds do, and together
comprise an atmosphere,
our place. What else is new?
A broom for you, a stack of rags

for me, our own old T-shirts cut
to squares and once again of use.
A tin of wax, these lovely smells:
tropic resins, petroleum.

To the Engraver of My Skin

I understand the pact is mortal,
agree to bear this permanence.

I contract with limitation; I say
no and no then yes to you, and sign

—here, on the dotted line—
for whatever comes, I do: our time,

our outline, the filling-in of our details
(it's density that hurts, always,

not the original scheme). I'm here
for revision, discoloration; here to fade

and last, ineradicable, blue. Write me!
This ink lasts longer than I do.

Principalities of June

Original light broke apart,
the Gnostics say,
when time began,

singular radiance
fractioned into form
—an easy theory

to believe,
in early summer,
when that first performance

seems repeated daily.
Though wouldn't it mean
each fracturing took us

that much further
from heaven?
Not in this town,

not in June: harbor
and cloudbank, white houses'
endlessly broken planes,

a long argument
of lilac shadows and whites
as blue as noon:

phrasebooks of day,
articulated most of all
in these roses,

which mount and swell
in dynasties of bloom,
their easy idiom

a soundless compaction
of lip on lip. Their work,
these thick flowerheads?

Built to contain
sunlight, they interrupt
that movement just enough

to transfix in air, at eye level,
now: held still, and shattering,
which is the way with light:

the more you break it
the nearer it comes to whole.

Summer Landscape

—Stuart Davis

This happy bit of Modernism could almost be
our town—white houses' simple geometry

complexified by scatter, angles of roofs
and fences, one cheerful tree, a yellow band

of dunes. A rippling harbor interpenetrates
everything: watery planes between scribbled clouds,

jumble of masts and riggings, spars,
blue surface, black dinghy, this shingled expanse

of shadow, and he's even painted around his Cubist
seaside town a border, each side a different color

(pink and black, yellow and fence-picket white)
as if to emphasize how firmly this place

is framed, known through all the art
that's been made of it, till it's a painting of itself:

light heightened and arranged. Exactly
what our town's been doing, these new-season days

out to impress with the sheer bravado
of what the atmosphere's done this time.

Yesterday a final slant of afternoon lit up
with heart-firing warmth the rusting side

of a white boat tied to the town pier.
Heaven, just then, and something like

the way a familiar face flares present
in candlelight, depths made clear

in the slightest flame . . . Then gone, leaving
a plain white flank starred with rust,

perfectly handsome but nothing to shout about
—as people actually did, walking on Commercial,

when they saw the harbor bathed in rose.
Weeks now, on the spire of the Unitarian Universalist

Meeting House, a red scaffolding's ringed
the crown, square-boned New England earnestness

gaining a jaunty bit of costume:
our spire disguised, for the season,

as a minaret, or a lighthouse in Alexandria,
or the high tower room of some exiled sultan's

fabled realm . . . What a little bit of red can do!
Inside, whale-tooth medallions jewel

the pews, and walls and ceiling deceive
with ornate grisaille, the trompe l'oeil work

of a genius architectural painter
passing through, who drew a hundred years

of eyes up the long lines of his false columns
to the gorgeous details of his false vault

—over which the steeple climbs like a steamstack
into the blue. I keep imagining, every day,

walking by, how the view from up there would tumble
in a density of gardens and dormers, our rooftops

splayed in fractal array. The perfect place,
if it were our work in the world simply to attend

to light, these shows given hourly—
Look now: that ultraviolet curtain's drawn,

and phantom stagehands trundle from the wings
a bank of shade, looming, cloud-belly blue.

Scratch that; here's a sudden wash of sun,
classical in its severity, striking all shadows

from the stage. I have a friend, Jade, a carpenter
who goes about her work in silver bangles,

bracelets overlaid on each arm, which seem
as much part of her tool kit as hammer

and pry bar and her marine-blue pickup truck.
Dependable and brave, she flashes in the sun,

mornings, when she mounts the steeple,
which now is scraped to nude intensity,

pine planks breathing salt air again,
shed of their pickling paint. Her task:

the regilding of the acanthus, our spire's
once-golden flourish angling up into summer air.

Who knew? All these years it's been a briny,
verdigrised blue, but Jade restores it to a luster

unremembered here. She poses high above
the woodblock print of a town, the steady, chilly harbor,

and anchors to the sturdy tip a crown.

Lily and Bronze

Zenith June and this tower:
seventeen white throats
opening a tier at a time

to interiors purely narcotic—

I mean the lily's giddy spire,
each trumpet nothing
but intent to drench

in scent and pollen
any approaching face.
Look at them,

the full flare of them,
and your looking empties out;

turn back and there they are
blazing: they go on arriving,
as if nothing ended but our attention.

Like those horses in Venice,
the Quadriga, four Roman bronzes
stolen to Constantinople,

robbed again to Venice,
mounted on the façade of the basilica
a thousand years

then brought in from
the chemical rain,
restless and looming

in a brick vault I entered
through a little door—
I, I say, but I wasn't then,

but suddenly bright faces tilted
just to one side, turbulent, breathing
and o for the speech to make you

the muscle and push of it,
a bronze mouth for the heft
and thunderhead,

sweat and fierce of them—

It's the same with the lilies:
look hard enough and they hurry
ceaseless toward a place where

you are no longer standing,
their flanks also dusted
in scoured gold. Seconds only,

until the moment collapses
and you turn away. Though
they go on unfolding,

in a great arrested suspension: leap and stasis fused.

After the Fourth

Bunting still billows on the hardware store,
neon glowers on the Lobster Pot. Marine awnings,
clapboards in their summer whites:

the whole town sagging a little, the day after,
leaning back, unbuttoned, too hot to touch.
Summer's settled now on a single plan,

gorgeous decline. The season's major sellers:
Off!, T-shirts, frozen stuff in all varieties
fat-free. We crowd together (is what we do

also what we are?) in the street, we flash
and school like smelts. Last night fireworks
rattled the windows and shook the pier

—brief thunder, since the Selectmen chose,
this year, to sink their funds into spectacle.
Every dog in town shook beneath beds and sofas

when the conclusive burst rained terror
and tympany. What did the gulls make of it,
adrift on their strand in the harbor?

(I love the nuanced, midnight vocabulary
of their cries.) Or seals who swam among
the sodden remnants, charred casings

fallen from heaven? They've mostly gone
north, to Maine or Nova Scotia, but a few
dazed stragglers blaze like dandelion heads

in the early sun, at land's end,
where wavelets pause for breath
between each frothing collapse. There,

near dawn, swam jellyfish
of a horrifying red, escaped Victorian curtains
trailing ferocious tatters,

whips and fringes pulsing freely,
electrically—lion's manes, they're called,
blown from tropic waters, and beaten,

in our shoals, to a menstrual pulp,
those who came too close,
while the rest hurried their blood clouds

away from shore, further, outward,
to rimless salinity, a Martian moon-disc
flotilla half wrecked, numberless:

We flare and fail in shallows,
burn in the liquid open.
A wild deep current brought us.

American Sublime

St. Johnsbury, Vermont

Closing time at the Athenaeum,
but this visitor bat
(who knows how he got in)
seems intent on staying the night;
our waving arms, a rolled *Times*,
the janitor's broom haven't fazed him a bit.

In flits and starts he swoops
in crazy eights from cornice to
pilaster, chandelier to book-
shelf top, finial to plaster-
work to pediment. He seems
especially to like the vast

painting he skims like a pond,
a Bierstadt prospect of Yosemite,
billboard for immensity. The painter's
out to correct our sense of scale:
grandeur meant not to diminish
but enlarge, as the eye hurries

up that cleft dome of rock
to hazy light, light made material,
crown of glory, a suffused
atmosphere intended to mean
intensely. Our adventurer
doesn't stop to look, careening

above this antique ad for fresh air
as though he owned it,
and these books and music stands
and brass easels which display
last century's genre paintings
leaning back, labeled, heavily framed.

What's more out of date, nature
or the representation of it?
A velvet dust-rag wing
brushes canvas, granite dome,
the varnished vastness,
then rests a beat on that bust of

—Emerson? And now we
visitors, though we've all enjoyed
the unexpected fluttery show,
give up. Time to go home.
Where did we park? Dim the lamps.
Last glance: bat and Bierstadt

all in the dark. Nothing. No,
there he is! Flying, just visible
in the faint signal of the exit sign:
our little hero circumambulating still
the gloss of oil, the polished pools
and waterfall, our rocks and rills.

Time on Main

Johnson, Vermont

The Masonic Temple—
white clapboard,
   columns straight
from some Egyptian opera set—

   began in resolution,
but settled
   to something jaunty,
accommodating time.

   The half-cocked
steeple's clock
   permanently stopped
at quarter past twelve.

   Noon? Midnight?
Whatever; it has two
   accurate moments
—a kind of achievement,

   after all these years.
The living Masons
   must be few, and wise,
here in the plain north,

   to keep a staunch
white meetinghouse

to disguise their treasury
of costume: luscious getups,

staffs and turbans
and robes, ritual fabrics
    of dream. Three steeples rise
from Main Street's sleep,

each one pointless:
this homage to Luxor,
    then a dour
Congregationalist stack,

then this: above
arched windows inscribed
    in marbled glass
LOOK UP, a little Delphi's

hung against the sky,
twelve columns squared
    around an open shaft
of pure New England air.

Below's a spate of retail,
equally dreamy:
    a new trinket shoppe,
Gifts for the Soul.

Black block letters
— BRAD'S HOUSE OF TIME—
    ring a neon clock.
In the cemetery, a hillock

where two routes
converge, flat slate
    markers lean in rows,
delicately inscribed:

urns and winged
skulls, willows bent
    in perennial grief.
All answered, somehow,

    by one man's stone
engraved in cursive
    with a motto
and farewell: *It's all right.*

    Time, I'd like to think
he meant, his hour,
    and ours, here in Egypt,
Vermont, Greece . . . Imagine

    thinking the passage
of time all right!
    A proposition this town
considers still, all night,

    the moon a delicious
frazzle in the rapids
    by the shut-down mill,
caught like Main,

    riddled with history,
and outside it,
    sending these spires
up into October,

    year after year,
at quarter past the hour.

Source

I'd been traveling all day, driving north
—smaller and smaller roads, clapboard houses
startled awake by the new green around them—

when I saw three horses in a fenced field
by the narrow highway's edge: white horses,

two uniformly snowy, the other speckled
as though he'd been rolling in flakes of rust.
They were of graduated sizes

—small, medium, large—and two stood
to watch while the smallest waded

up to his knees in a shallow pond,
tossing his head and taking
—it seemed unmistakable—delight

in the cool water around his hooves
and ankles. I kept on driving, I went into town

to visit the bookstores and the coffee bar,
and looked at the new novels
and the volumes of poetry, but all the time

it was horses I was thinking of,
and when I drove back to find them

the three companions left off
whatever it was they were playing at,
and came nearer the wire fence—

I'd pulled over onto the grassy shoulder
of the highway—to see what I'd brought them.

Experience is an intact fruit,
core and flesh and rind of it; once cut open,
entered, it can't be the same, can it?

Though that is the dream of the poem:
as if we could look out

through that moment's blushed skin.
They wandered toward the fence.
The tallest turned toward me;

I was moved by the verticality of her face,
elongated reach from the ear-tips

down to white eyelids and lashes,
the pink articulation
of nostrils, wind stirring the strands

of her mane a little to frame the gaze
in which she fixed me. She was the bold one;

the others stood at a slight distance
while she held me in her attention.
Put your tongue to the green-flecked

peel of it, reader, and taste it
from the inside: Would you believe me
if I said that beneath them a clear channel

ran from the three horses to the place
they'd come from, the cool womb

of nothing, cave at the heart
of the world, deep and resilient and firmly set
at the core of things? Not emptiness,

not negation, but a generous, cold nothing:
the breathing space out of which new shoots

are propelled to the grazing mouths,
out of which horses themselves are tendered
into the new light. The poem wants the impossible;

the poem wants a name for the kind nothing
at the core of time, out of which the foals

come tumbling: curled, fetal, dreaming,
and into which the old crumple, fetlock
and skull breaking like waves of foaming milk . . .

Cold, bracing nothing, which mothers forth
mud and mint, hoof and clover, root-hair

and horse-hair and the accordion bones
of the rust-spotted little one unfolding itself
into the afternoon. You too: you flare

and fall back into the necessary
open space. What could be better than that?

It was the beginning of May,
the black earth nearly steaming,
and a scatter of petals decked the mud

like pearls, everything warm with setting out,
and you could see beneath their hooves
the path they'd traveled up, the horse-road

on which they trot into the world, eager for pleasure
and sunlight, and down which they descend,

in good time, into the source of spring.